A COASTAL PASSAGE

A COASTAL PASSAGE

AN ARTIST'S VIEW OF THE ENGLISH COASTLINE

DAVID C. BELL

SWAN·HILL
PRESS

Acknowledgements

Mr & Mrs Rainthorpe

Mr R Perry

Mr C Harrison

Mr & Mrs R Parker

John Good

Medite Shipping Co (UK) Ltd

Felixstowe Dock and Railway Co.

MEDITE SHIPPING COMPANY (U.K.) Ltd.

First published in the UK in 1999
by Swan Hill Press, an imprint of Airlife Publishing Ltd

British Library Cataloguing-in-Publication Data
   A catalogue record for this book
   is available from the British Library

ISBN 1 84037 087 4

Typeset by Servis Filmsetting Ltd
Printed in Hong Kong

Swan Hill Press
an imprint of Airlife Publishing Ltd
101 Longden Road, Shrewsbury, SY3 9EB, England
E-mail: airlife@airlifebooks.com
Website: www.airlifebooks.com

Introduction

It has been my ambition for some years, to gather together a collection of paintings and drawings of England's coastline. The majority of artists gain some degree of satisfaction from exhibiting their works. I feel however, that as valuable as the gallery or exhibition may be, it represents a very fragmented view of any artist's work. I have therefore chosen to use this book as a showcase for a sequence of drawings, sketches and paintings completed over some twenty years, in the field and studio, to give a more complete view of my work depicting England's coastline.

Just as an historian's work is of little value without reference to the present day, I feel that any artistic representation of England's rich and varied coastline is made all the more interesting by looking back on its history. Thus the theme throughout this book is of past and present.

In England we are extremely lucky in that wherever our homes may be we are never more than a few hours drive from the sea. Also, because of England's geological and social history, anyone wishing to paint a coastal scene can, within the space of sixty minutes or so, find precipitous cliffs and esturine mudflats or small indented coves in close proximity to bustling ports. Thus there is a wealth of inspirational source material close to hand whatever your inclination as an artist. Similarly, the craft visiting our shores include huge ocean liners and small working craft like the Hastings fishing boats and the cobles of the East Coast.

I do not intend this book to be a gazetteer or journal but hopefully an encouragement to anyone who enjoys our maritime heritage or has the desire to capture maritime subjects in brush or pen.

The dimensions of paintings and sketches given in the captions are in inches, without frame and width × depth.

Foreword

This is an outstanding collection of images of England's coastline, both past and present, by a skilled and perceptive artist. We constantly hear of the decline of the merchant fleet and this is certainly true, numerically, as more and more vessels are 'flagged out'. Britain, however, is still very much a maritime nation and through travel by ferry and the ever growing number of small-boatmen (and women) more people than ever before have some very real and direct contact with the sea.

The artist has depicted images of our coastal towns and villages – ports, harbours and creeks – both as they are now and as they were in the past. In so doing he demonstrates the immense variety of craft, often unique to a particular region, which have sailed from our shores over the centuries. A surprising number of older types are still to be found in use, some little altered like the Yorkshire coble, others like the Hastings lugger are somewhat modernised. These traditional craft are a stark contrast to the strange and ultra-modern forms of the catamaran ferries which operate from Folkestone and south coast ports or the Isle of Man.

For many years, David Bell concentrated on water-colour and this is possibly his preferred medium. Drawings certainly constitute the bulk of the reproductions in this volume though in latter years he has also become adept with oil paints, as exemplified by the Scarborough painting *After the great gale*. This painting recreates a scene of bygone times which can be contrasted with the images of the present.

Always informative, his work reflects not only a keen eye with many years' observation of the sea and ships, but also practical experience as a former officer in the Merchant Navy. After eight years at sea he studied at the Hull College of Art before embarking on a career as a full-time professional artist. David's understanding is both that of the artist and the sailor, and he has explored the east coast of England not only from the shore side but also by frequent coastwise cruising.

He has always been interested in the history of his subjects and the development of marine art, an inclination he pursued whilst at college. He was captivated by the great Hull tradition which began in the eighteenth century and produced artists of the stature of John Ward (1798–1849), Thomas Somerscales (1842–1927) and Harry Hudson Rodmell (1896–1984) and he now continues this unbroken chain into the twenty-first century. As with these artists of old, 'ship portraits' form a significant part of his output, such as images of the *Norland* used in the Falkland campaign, the *Sir Walter Raleigh* floating headquarters of Operation *Raleigh* and his great favourites, the Humber ferries, particularly the *Lincoln Castle*.

A series of oil commissions of lifeboats, including *Bridlington*, *Spurn*, *Guernsey* and *Alderney*, have been sold in print form to raise funds for the RNLI (Royal National Lifeboat Institution). A series of commissioned paintings for the Armed Forces in 1984 led to a five-week painting trip in the Falklands, producing work in a very demanding environment. In 1985, a one-man show in Beverley was a showcase for a collection of water-colours and drawings. Three years later, the same venue displayed a variety of maritime subjects in oils. He has also had shows in Hull, Ireland and Canada and has contributed to prestigious London exhibitions. David is the author of *Britain's Maritime History* which contains pencil, ink and water-colour drawings illustrating vessels through the ages from the reign of Elizabeth Tudor to the present century.

It has been a great privilege to write this foreword, having followed with the greatest interest and delight the development of his artistic talent as it has unfolded since his student days. This volume is a real breath of salt air and will provide immense pleasure to those who love being afloat or simply enjoy watching the daily toing and froing of big ships and small boats, mixed with the tang of seaweed and Stockholm tar. It will transport armchair travellers to their favourite river and seaside places, and encourage them to further explore the many miles of English coastline whenever the opportunity arises.

Arthur Credland
Hull Maritime Museum

The starting point . . .
Northumberland, Holy Island to Amble

Loading Lime, Holy Island 1860. Water-colour, 15in x 8in.

8

Longstones Lighthouse 1980. Water-colour, 9in x 6in.

Lindisfarne Castle. Water-colour, 6in x 4in.

Foreshore, Lindisfarne. Water-colour, 4in x 4in.

Lindisfarne Castle. Water-colour, 9in x 6in.

I've chosen the wonderfully rugged and appealing coastline of Northumberland as the starting point of this first collection of paintings and drawings. Between the grey fortified stonework of Berwick and the stunning charm of Warkworth lies a coast of unrivalled beauty, unpopulated and unspoilt.

On a clear day it is a shoreline of space and solitude. The wide and sandy bays are punctuated with rugged coastal villages, fashioned by the unforgiving attentions of the North Sea. There are several gems to visit for the artist and tourist alike, and more through good luck than good planning, most of the painting trips I've made to this county have been during clement weather, and as the drawings show, Holy Island has received the most attention.

Lindisfarne is, without doubt, an area of aesthetic and spiritual beauty. The causeway linking Lindisfarne with the mainland seems to keep it at arm's length from the commercialism and the undesirable elements of the present day. Only the sight of a monk doing his weekly shopping spoils the feeling that Lindisfarne is suspended in a time warp. The island was the home of Celtic Christianity and some of the ancient peace and calm still pervades the few streets that criss-cross this much-visited landmark.

Approaching Lindisfarne along the causeway when the tide is right, one cannot fail to be impressed by the sight of the relatively small and still occupied castle rising majestically on a rocky outcrop. Further investigation around the bay on foot reveals the long rocky beach, punctuated by old and weathered wooden posts close to the castle's shore, the remnants of a working jetty. Indeed, below the castle are well preserved lime-kilns, which show how this source of income was worked for shipment to places like Dundee. In the sepia drawing, I've depicted a typical schooner at the jetty loading lime circa 1860.

Not far away, and visible from Lindisfarne, is Bamburgh Castle, an impressive structure standing on the edge of the Great Whin Sill, guarding its stretch of coastline. I sketched this fortress from the village side, showing the sheer rocky base. I then crossed the dunes onto the beach to the north and painted a small water-colour, which shows only a hint of its powerful presence.

Southwards, is the charming and peaceful harbour of Alnmouth, taking its name from the River Aln which meets the sea at this point and once served as the port of Alnwick. Once you have by necessity traversed the shoreline golf-course and met the North Sea head on, you can walk round the estuary, on an ebb tide of course, and find excellent viewpoints for painting and drawing.

Bamburgh Castle, a view from the sports field. Water-colour, 7in x 7in.

Bamburgh Castle 1980. Water-colour, 12in x 6in.

Dunstanburgh Castle. Water-colour, 10in x 7in.

Choosing a location for this drawing I couldn't, in the time available, find a satisfying focal point and decided on a broader view from the bottom of a farm track. For me this was a hurried picture, and I felt I should have spent more time finding a sounder viewpoint. This initial visit did, however, result in a welcome familiarity on my return. Often, it is desirable to visit more than once before committing brush to paper.

Alnmouth Estuary 1983. Water-colour, 18in x 9in.

Further down the coast, the friendly port of Amble has obviously changed from its prosperous coal-exporting past to a slowly modernising but quiet fishing community. The harbour, or rather the meandering River Coquet, was re-aligned in the 1840s by the erection of large stone piers north and south of the estuary to help the flow of the river and establish a harbour that could principally ship out the locally mined coal. Quays and staithes were built on the south side and, quite impressively, coal could be loaded directly from the railway trucks into the waiting vessels. From a peak in the thirties to a rapid decline in the sixties, the staithes and railways had amazingly disappeared by 1970. As with the demise of many of our ports and harbours, it is hard to believe the great volume of shipping and commercial activity that went on at Amble compared with the present day scene of neglected piers and negligible shipping.

The sepia drawing is of Amble or rather Warkworth and Amble Harbour at the turn of the century, viewed from what is now the marina. A short walk of about half a mile from here along the river bank provided the viewpoint for the water-colour of Warkworth Castle.

Warkworth and Amble Harbour c1900. Water-colour, 17in x 10in.

Warkworth Castle. Water-colour, 16in x 10in.

. . . and on to Yorkshire from Whitby to the Humber

Traders of Whitby c1885. Water-colour, 24in x 18in.

Whitby still retains the remarkable charm of an old sea port. As someone who has lived in Yorkshire and sailed out of this historic port, it still holds the same special magnetism for me that it did on my first visit many years ago. I have visited Whitby time and time again, never failing to find some aspect to capture and record.

The marina, Humber Dock, Hull. Ink, 13in x 10in.

The port at the mouth of the River Esk is basically composed of two halves, both seemingly unrelated. Once you have found a place to park you can venture along the harbour's west bank from the swing-bridge down the usually congested harbourside through, or around, the fish market, and look down at the fishing craft discharging their cargoes as they have done for centuries. Alternatively, you can simply take in the views. The remains of the fishing fleet somewhat incongruously share the harbour side with the candy-floss, amusements and 'Dracula experience' of a more modern Whitby. A walk along the west pier is rewarded by views of old Whitby on the one hand and the mixed moods of the North Sea on the other. To the north the miles of Upgang Beach stretch towards the appropriately named headland of Sandsend.

Looking at the east aspect of Whitby, the shape and structure of the waterfront façade must look today much as it did a century ago. The colliers and traders of the past have been replaced by a few yachts and the R.N.L.I. lifeboat, and on an ebb tide the occasional fishing boat or pleasure craft hauled up on the mud for repair.

Study for 'Whitby's Heritage'. Water-colour, 10in x 7in.

Staithes Harbour, low tide. Water-colour, 10in x 4in.

Like Staithes and Runswick to the north and Robin Hood's Bay to the south, visiting Old Town Whitby with its inherent atmosphere, close-knit houses and narrow cobbled roads evokes the old mariner's lifestyle. A stroll out onto Fish Pier or the adjacent Tate Hill provides an ideal spot for sketching. The early pencil drawing of the Esk was done from here and shows the local dredger moored waiting for the right conditions to work. The water-colour *Traders of Whitby* is an imagined view that I'm sure would have been seen regularly on a ebb tide and, more often than not, on a misty morning. This is set in the lower harbour, looking east.

The Esk, Whitby. Pencil, 12in x 7in.

Low water, Whitby 1995. Water-colour, 15in x 18in.

Beached Brig, Filey c1880. Oil, 36in x 24in.

Runswick Bay. Ink, 9in x 6in.

Local Fisherman arriving at Whitby 1988. Water-colour, 18in x 11in.

The harbour, Scarborough 1977. Water-colour, 16in x 8in.

After the Great Storm, Scarborough South Beach 1880. Oil, 36in x 24in.

Further south, the holiday town of Scarborough has an interesting mixture of commerce, with its small fishing fleet and visiting coasters, and the hustle and bustle of the popular seaside town. The small water-colour sketch, one of the oldest in the book, was produced sometime in the summer of 1978 amidst the boats of the harbour. Ten years later when I became reasonably competent with oils, I painted the scene shown here based on the Great Storm of 1880. Under sail and in bad weather this coastline can be very hostile at any time, and in October 1880 an easterly gale drove many vessels ashore, which had been either taking shelter in the bay or making for the harbour. The painting shows the possible scene the next day in the south bay, looking north towards the castle.

Southwards, in my native Hull, I can recall memorable scenes outside my pre-sea training school, Trinity House. Prince's Dock was bustling with trawlers being fitted out and finished – a scene reflected in many other ports around the country at that time. However, what is so poignant to me about these recollections is that fifteen years later whilst at art college, I would not only be spending time sketching and painting on the River Hull, the pier and on the docks, but also drawing and recording these very same vessels being cut up and scrapped down at Draper's Yard on the Humber foreshore. Perhaps this is what inspired the idea of this book, the fact that much of our maritime heritage was disappearing at the hands of 'progress' and needed to be recorded.

Draper's Yard, Hull 1977. Water-colour, 7in x 6in.

Lord Lloyd. *Water-colour, 5in x 7in.*

The painting *Home and away* shows two pre-war 'side-winder' trawlers arriving and departing on the Humber, not far from the old St Andrew's fish dock. On the left, arriving, is the *Cape Portland* built at Selby in 1936, and to the right the *Arctic Explorer*, also built at Selby in 1937, is leaving for northern fishing grounds.

In the mid-sixties, I occasionally fished in the Humber, off King George Dock, with friends from school, always arriving very early in the morning. I never fathomed why I always arrived so early until writing this. If you were early and stayed a long time, at some point the tide would be right for the memorable sight of a steady stream of trawlers departing the Humber. This was usually for a three-week round fishing trip in northern waters, with trawlers coming home on the flood-tide with a catch for the waiting market.

Home and away, Hull trawlers 1938. Water-colour, 19in x 11in.

Paddle steamer Lincoln Castle, *dry-dock, Hull. Water-colour, 18in x 12in.*
Private collection.

Northern Desire, *Hull Docks. Water-colour, 8in x 5in.*

Study of St Andrew's Dock, Hull 1950s. Water-colour, 13in x 8in.

In the days when the Humber was bustling with trade from fishing to emigration, any prospective artist would have had a tremendous choice of subject matter. However, today activity is mainly concentrated on the few big ships visiting King George Dock. As trade declined, particularly the fishing industry, the Humber became a very different river. The artist has to be more inquisitive and inventive, and perhaps have more vision in selecting a subject. The Albert and William Wright Docks are now home to the small remaining fishing fleet. Comprising a variety of fishing and related vessels, shown here is an ex-stern trawler the *Northern Desire*, now (or at the time I saw it) a Fisheries Patrol Vessel. The appealing air of haphazardness makes for a more unusual scene and certainly provides scope for an artistic eye. The 1975 River Hull painting is sadly typical. Today this scene has been cleansed and rejuvenated, making it quite unattractive for the artist.

River Hull 1975. Water-colour, 26in x 20in. Private collection.

Humber lifeboat, off Flamborough. Oil, 36in x 24in. Private collection.

Below is one of the dozens of sketches I've made over the years of the P.S. *Lincoln Castle*. I first travelled on it as a small child and then regularly when I attended Trinity House Navigation School in Hull. Built in Glasgow in 1940 for service between Hull and New Holland, her long working life came to a slightly premature end when boiler replacement and the building of the Humber Bridge in 1981 terminated her sailing days. But fate was kind to her and she can now be seen in Alexandra Dock in Grimsby, her original port of registration. She is my favourite vessel.

I don't have a great deal of work portraying Lincolnshire, but I'm fortunate to be able to sail regularly from the marina in Grimsby, and have included some recent drawings and water-colours of the fish dock and slipway appearing much the same today as they did in the 1920s.

Manxman, *Hull Docks 1995. Water-colour, 9in x 8in.*

Paddle steamer Lincoln Castle. *Pencil, 10in x 7in.*

Slipways, Grimsby fish docks, 1996. Pencil, 12in x 8in.

Spurn Lighthouse. Sepia drawing, 9in x 6in.

Ross Tiger, *Alexandra Dock, Grimsby. Water-colour, 10in x 6in.*

'CITY OF EDINBURGH' (HULL)
- FISH DOCK - GRIMSBY

Sketches of Grimsby Docks. Pencil, 16in x 12in.

The Slipways, Grimsby fish dock 1935. Water-colour, 15in x 10in.

A busy tide, Humber estuary 1931. Water-colour, 19in x 12in.

. . . in Norfolk from King's Lynn to Cley next the Sea

Custom House, King's Lynn. Water-colour, 11in x 7in.

Cley Mill. Sepia drawing, 8in x 8in.

Both the drawings produced here of King's Lynn were actually painted from the opposite bank over at West Lynn. It is a rather featureless riverside but the small water-colour sketch shows its one outstanding feature, the Custom House, originally built in 1683 as a Merchant Exchange. Just along the riverbank and painted from the same spot on the same day is Lynn's small but colourful fishing fleet.

Cley Mill 1984. Water-colour, 8in x 6in.

Fishermen, King's Lynn. Sepia drawing, 11in x 5 in.

Not quite town-size but a place of character, Wells-next-the-Sea is a lively mix of tourists, fishing boats and an active and commercial quayside. In fact, the quayside is another place that changes dramatically from high to low tide. One minute it's all water and activity and the next everything is high and dry and definitely out of use. It is always a pleasant place to visit and admire at leisure, and of course sketch. Indeed, the rare sight of a sailing vessel working its way onto the quayside on a high tide makes a sketchbook entry essential. The *Albatross* was, at the time I saw it, one of the few (if not the only) sailing traders working out of the U.K. With its cargo of soya beans it is a regular visitor to this peaceful coastline.

Wells-next-the-Sea. Pencil drawing, 11in x 5in.

*Fisherman under repair, Brancaster
Staithe. Water-colour, 8in x10in.*

'ALBATROSS'
WELLS · NEXT · THE · SEA 1994

Albatross, *Wells-next-the-Sea. Water-colour, 7in x 8in.*

The serenity of the Norfolk coastline in particular gives an effortless air to a painting. However, the northern coastline is a little monotonous in features and so a slight incursion inland to Cley next the Sea was made. Cley is no longer next to the sea and hasn't been since the surrounding marshland was reclaimed in the seventeenth century; the waves are now forced to break on a shingle bank a mile away from this ancient shoreline. Many years ago I produced this small sketch in my car of a famous and appealing eighteenth century mill on a track leading to the beach on the south side. The mill is situated on the edge of the marsh overlooking the River Glaven. Along with Blakeney and Wiveton, Cley was once a thriving navigable port trading with the Low Countries.

However, silting has now deprived all these sites of any maritime trade. The sepia painting on page 36 is from the west of the windmill, showing the mill, quay and the Glaven at low tide, at the turn of the century. The panoramic painting of the mill is a much more recent depiction, with a viewpoint from close to the tidal barrier bank, looking westwards. This is a much better composition and contrasts with the sepia drawing, but it should have been a little bigger and painted much more quickly. As with most of my work I sketched it out meticulously before starting to paint, but ran out of time before being able to get anywhere near finishing it in one day. I therefore lost the immediacy of the work and had to finish the detail of the mill in the studio.

The white racing boats, Brancaster. Water-colour, 9in x 6in.

Cley Mill 1996. Water-colour, 17in x 12in.

This area is definitely the most difficult with which to demonstrate a contrast over the last century. Little can have changed as there is little to change in the way of harbours and jetties or any general modernisation, or perhaps I am tempting providence. Although the water-colour *Boats at Brancaster Straithe* looks like a scene from years ago it is actually quite recent. I'm not sure what kind of fishing boat it was, possibly a mussel boat, but it was another timeless scene. *Fisherman under repair* (see page 39) and the sketches show the more modern versions of these fishing boats, some modern and redundant or just abandoned, and all lying around the creeks and waterways between Brancaster and Wells.

Boat study, Wells. 6in x 4in.

Boat study, Brancaster. 6in x 9in.

Idle boats, Mow Creek, Brancaster Staithe. Water-colour, 13in x 9in.

Moston Creek. Water-colour, 13in x 7in.

Boat study.

. . . and into Suffolk, from Lowestoft to Felixstowe

A century ago East Anglia's main industry was agriculture. The growth of cereal supplied the many tide-mills and maltings. Grain was processed to supply the breweries, and the barge was the most important means of transport in both collection and distribution. Sadly, the arrival of the railways ended this trade. Though the quay at Snape closed, the Maltings survived intact and is now used for a variety of enterprises, none more important or famous than serving as the home of the Aldeburgh Festival of Music.

In the past I've sailed up the River Ore to Orford and from there up the River Alde as far as the delightful town of Aldeburgh, but to paint the scene here of the Maltings I arrived at Snape more conventionally by car on a very dull day. Personally, to achieve some success, I need to be interested in a subject, whether it's a recreated historical subject or a record of the present day. I also try to give a lot of consideration to the choice of subjects and the end result I want to achieve. Now, after some years and many attempts at painting different though mainly maritime subjects, it's now become second nature to constantly scan any scene for shape and colour, for detail and interest. With an element of luck, this usually results in a successful painting. Though light and atmosphere are vital ingredients in a painting I nevertheless tackled the Maltings. This became a challenging painting on an overcast day, forcing me to work hard on the contrast of the white boat against the warm brick buildings in order to give visual appeal and to compensate for the flat light. The difficulty was resisting my natural tendency to overwork the subject.

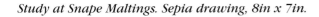

Study at Snape Maltings. Sepia drawing, 8in x 7in.

Zebu. Alongside the quay, Snape Maltings. Water-colour, 17in x 12in.

A study of a sailing trawler and a steam drifter, 6in x 3in.

Morning sail, trawlers leaving Lowestoft c1900. Water-colour, 17in x 10in.

Modern fisherman, Lowestoft. Line and wash, 8in x 6in.

A combination of commercial shipping, fishing, oil-rig support and the established holiday resort makes Lowestoft a coastal town with a split personality. The distinction is made clear on walking down the south pier with the unchanged sandy beaches and throngs of holidaymakers stretching endlessly to the south, the pier fishermen in the middle taking the opportunity of a high tide, and then the modern North Sea industries to the north. The stark utilitarian fishing boats with highly visible orange bridges and modern gear combined with the shapeless modern day coaster emerging from the dock make an interesting scene. However, I need the lure of a polished deck or wooden handrail to keep my sketchbook open. Nevertheless, the water-colour of the Lowestoft trawlers sailing out of the piers was developed from the model boats and photographs found in the charming museum to the north of the town, and is a sharp contrast to the modern freezing and packing industries found across the road today.

Fishing gear, Lowestoft Harbour. Sepia drawing, 7in x 6in.

River sketches. Pencil, 13in x10in.

Gaff sailor, River Orwell. Water-colour, 8in x 9in.

Another fine place with two distinctive faces is the small Victorian holiday resort of Felixstowe. From a viewpoint in the 'old town' you can see a classic resort with wonderful seafront gardens, a promenade and pier but southwards towards Landguard Point is the other quite fascinating face of Felixstowe. If you can find your way to Landguard Fort you will enjoy the wonderful views and activities of the Orwell and Stour estuaries, with a glittering array of boats and yachtsmen usually 'giving way' to the box-like 'leviathans' constantly plying the buoyed channel. It is an easy place to walk about and sketch – I've even done large paintings from the car park during bad weather. Directly across the estuary is Harwich, a busy ferry port. Back on this side and up-river is the huge complex of Felixstowe's port, with its constant activity it is now of considerable importance to the imports and exports of the U.K.

M.S.C. Giovanna, Felixstowe. Water-colour, 6in x 5in.

Redundant lightships off Shotley Point. Water-colour, 14in x 9in.

Ivaran berthing, Felixstowe. Water-colour, 28in x 19in. Private collection.

Remains of the old pier, Felixstowe. Sepia drawing, 12in x 6in.

I've sailed many times up and down the Orwell, both north and south into the rivers, coves and creeks of these natural yet demanding yachting waters and, time permitting, have endeavoured to record all things nautical. The natural place to start at is Pin Mill, on the north side of Shotley peninsula. Down a narrow road, the flat muddy banks of the Orwell with its fascinating collection of boats, bits and pieces and natural backdrop is very inviting for any artist. The sepia drawing on page 55 shows just two of the many barges simply parked on the flat, muddy 'hard' of Pin Mill. There is a repair yard and chandlers for the yachtsman and barge owner, but there does seem to have been a slightly increasing air of neglect creeping in over the last few years. Perhaps it's just that less work is being carried out. To help out on a busy drawing day and encourage the artist to stay a while, there is always the welcoming and atmospheric pub, the 'Butt and Oyster', a watering-hole that must be known to mariners all over the world. The water-colour *Barges at Pin Mill*, though painted some years ago, is still a happy reminder of my first visit to this river.

M.S.C. Angela, *Felixstowe. Pencil, 7in x 6in.*

Marje, *River Orwell. Water-colour, 9in x 7in.*

Sketch page, around Felixstowe. 7in x 11in.

Barges under repair, Pin Mill hard. Water-colour, 19in x12in.

Pin Mill sketches. 16in x 11in.

Local barges, Pin Mill hard. Sepia study, 18in x 10in.

River sketches.

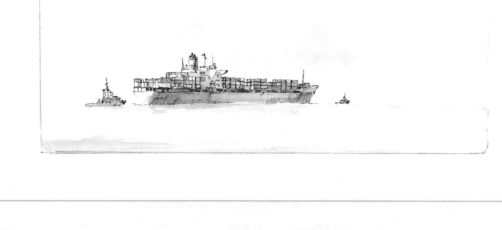

Beach scene, Walberswick. 10in x 5in.

. . . and on to Kent from Rochester to Folkestone

Rochester is my starting point and introduction to the varied and scenic coastline of Kent. I've visited the Kent coast many times before, not always to paint. Years ago, I sailed up the Medway as far as Kingsnorth, and thought a visit to historic Rochester would be a good start for a painting weekend. Once home to many spritsail barges and sailing vessels, Rochester, like all the ports, havens and creeks of the Kent coastline, is now of course devoid of such activity. That period of sail, now almost extinct, still holds a fascination for me as it does for many others, but there is still a pleasant atmosphere of tradition and everyday working life all along this coast which the artist can explore and illustrate.

River Medway, Rochester. Water-colour, 15in x 9in.

Artists down the years have chosen to paint the spritsail barge. I've always thought its appeal lay in its 'romance', in some ways similar to the landscape artists' 'horse and plough'. The popularity of the barge means many are preserved and fully operational. Personally, I think these boats are difficult to portray. Working with oils, I can get by but with water-colours I struggle with the deep red sails, though I dare say it is just my perception of them from 'reality to portrayal'. My usual solution is to view them from a more interesting angle, showing different sail combinations, especially when manoeuvring under sail and power. Having had the opportunity to sail from the Orwell for a few years I revelled in the opportunities to observe and sketch spritsail barges. The small painting of Rochester was produced at a quiet spot at the base of Rochester Bridge next to a carpenter's work shop. The spritsail barge was 'manoeuvred' by my eye to that position, but the rest was depicted as seen. The vessel in the background is the *Chrysanthemum*. Sadly, since this painting was completed she has been ravaged by fire and her future is uncertain.

Dry-dock, Chatham Dockyard. Water-colour, 9in x 13in.

H.M.S. Victory. *Sepia water-colour, 8in x 9in.*

Visiting Chatham Dockyard is a wonderful experience for landlubbers and seafarers alike. Couple that with palette, pen and paper and you have all the inspiration and subject matter you could wish for. Far too much exists at Chatman to do it justice in this first book, but its preservation and development into a 'living', 'working museum' has been remarkably well conceived and achieved. Chatham's most famous vessel, H.M.S. *Victory*, now preserved at Portsmouth, was built in No. 2 dock between 1759–65. The sepia drawing shows her not then but after a major refit at Chatham in 1803. In dramatic contrast is the water-colour (more than a morning's work) of a rather different vessel, which was high and dry on the stocks having its major refit and a lick of paint. This huge complex is a place to collect and record much authentic material and equally to stroll about for inspiration for an imaginary scene to paint.

Sittingbourne provides another gem for painters, a great contrast from Chatham Dockyard, at the Neptune Barge Museum and boatyard. To say that this is a sleepy boatyard is an understatement. The barges have an air of a long undisturbed slumber. On any day this boatyard affords the artist a tremendous opportunity to absorb the easy ambience, picking a spot to visualise all this potential and making a few translations onto paper.

On my only visit here I sketched for most of the day and decided on this view for a dramatic late afternoon scene with a low sun casting strong shadows, enhancing the shapes and colours already present. The water-colour shown here was studio finished but hopefully demonstrates the feeling of warmth and tranquillity exuded from this location.

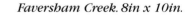

Faversham Creek. 8in x 10in.

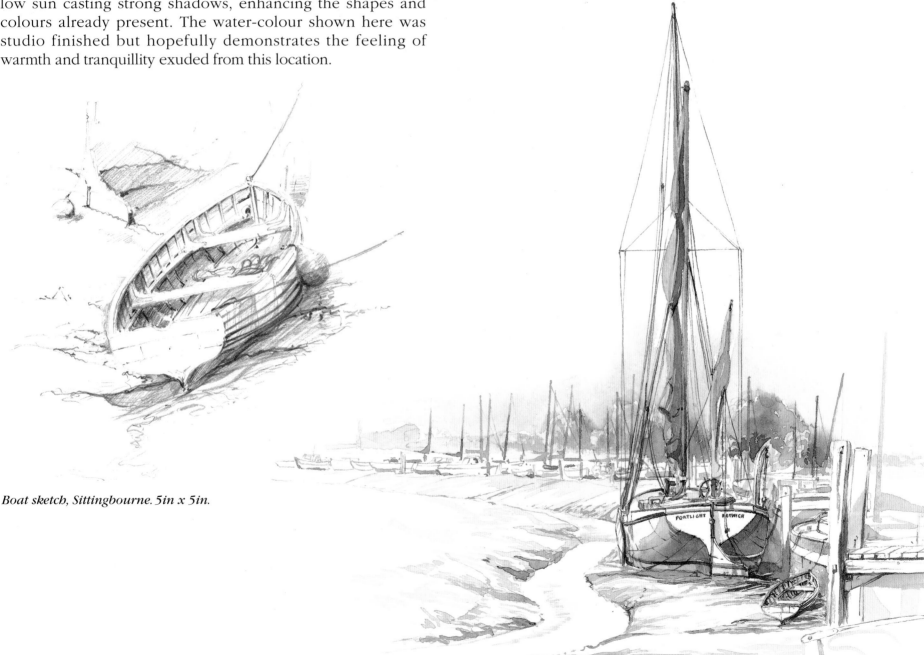

Boat sketch, Sittingbourne. 5in x 5in.

The Neptune boatyard, Sittingbourne. 17in x10in.

62

Sketch-book pages.

- Neptune's Yard -

Moving east, then south to the eastern seaboard of Kent, we arrive at Ramsgate. South-facing, it is one of those places that can give many hours of interest to all visitors. A busy harbour, it has commercial shipping, ferries, dredging, fishing, ship-repairing and a lifeboat, all set against the backdrop of Regency buildings. Like many ports, its origin was actually in fishing. Originally, Sandwich, one of the Cinque ports just inland and five miles upstream, was far more important until the Stour, though still navigable, silted up and Ramsgate Harbour was built at the end of the seventeenth century.

Observational drawing poses no problem when people and boats are static. However, at Ramsgate everything was non-stop action, and it was more tempting to watch rather than draw. Who can resist the character of a working dredger – fortunately for me this one was stationary for a long time, allowing a leisurely sketching session.

The sepia drawing of Ramsgate c1900 shows an imagined view of the harbour's west wall and lighthouse with a typical Ramsgate fishing smack outward bound, a scene typical of the end of the last century.

Sea-Cat manoeuvring, Folkestone. 12in x 6in.

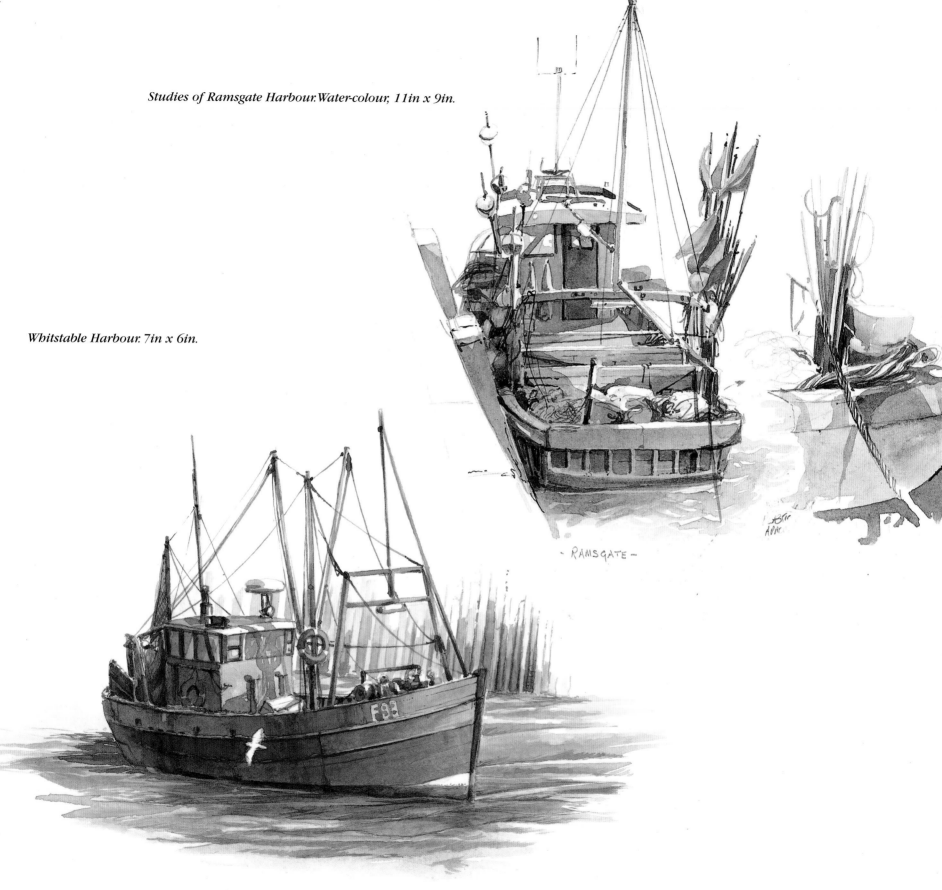

Studies of Ramsgate Harbour. Water-colour, 11in x 9in.

Whitstable Harbour. 7in x 6in.

- RAMSGATE -

Ramsgate Harbour c1900. 10in x 6in.

Walmer life boat house. Sepia water-colour, 8in x 6in.

Coastal scene, North Foreland. 7in x 6in.

Folkestone Harbour. Pen and ink, 15in x 11in.

. . . along to Sussex from Hastings to Newhaven

The Stade, Hastings. Sepia water-colour, 9in x 6in.

The Stade, Hastings 1996. 26in x 15in.

Boat study, Alexandra, *Hastings. Sepia, 6in x 9in.*

All along the south coast, the 'resort' seems to dominate the skyline as tourism and continental travel have become the main industry and fishing has been demoted to a minor role. Though I acknowledge the march of progress, I chose to start with Old Town Hastings, with its charming sprawl of old buildings and the fishing community. Like many ports-come-resorts that have an established tourist economy, trade and tourism can and does work side-by-side and nowhere more so than Hastings. With its unique working beach of new but traditionally designed craft, which have continued a certain way of life for two centuries or more, the Hastings fishing fleet has probably survived because it cannot change or evolve any more. That is to say the beach is a limited working area, the launching and beaching is carried out in a unique way and only the local grounds are fished. Many rival fishing ports have become fashionable resorts at the expense of their traditional fishing industry but the character of Hastings survives, so far.

Hauling boats, Hastings Beach. Water-colour, 9in x 13in.

This was my second painting trip to Hastings and I prepared a drawing for a large water-colour on the morning I arrived. My viewpoint was from the edge of the old breakwater to which I returned early the next morning to begin painting. It was an ideal misty morning with the low sun just breaking through, providing an atmospheric and inspiring vista. However, as my style involves a long series of washes it wasn't until ten or so that the sun was high enough to dry the paint quickly so that my progress could be more rapid. By that time I was ready for a break and walked amongst the boats for a closer look and to collect the detail for studio work. The results of my endeavours are shown here.

Sketches, Hastings. 16in x 10in.

Boat study, Hastings beach. Pencil, 9in x 7in.

Apart from work featuring Hastings, I didn't have a great deal of work from this coastline, recent or old. I tend to avoid the populated resorts, deliberately if I'm honest. The next place featured in my sketch-books, still in East Sussex, is Cuckmere Haven and also Newhaven. I remember having doubts about taking all my equipment on that long walk to the shoreline and wondering if it would be worth it. It wasn't, as it rained and rained. However, the Seven Sisters Cliffs are spectacular and must be worth a return visit.

Shipping on the River Ouse, Newhaven. Sepia, 12in x 8in.

Looking up river, Newhaven. Pencil, 12in x 6in.

View of Seven Sisters from Cuckmere Haven. Water-colour, 12in x 8in.

Newhaven provided my refuge and consequently I seem to have numerous sketches of what is a relatively small cross-channel port. The sepia drawing of Newhaven shows a brig on the River Ouse at the turn of the century, about to discharge at one of the small wooden jetties. The vessel would probably have had a cargo of coal for the ships on the established ferry service to the continent. These jetties still exist, albeit with some fresh timber, as can be seen from the other recent drawings, particularly the one with the tug and barge which features the same viewpoint used for the sepia drawing. The buildings in the background also still remain. On the opposite bank was what looked like the small ferry/cruise boat the *Southsea*. Some ten years earlier I was on this boat with my family leisurely plying the Solent. Now with its engines removed and funnels capped, its destiny looks sealed.

Shipping, old and new, Newhaven. Sepia, 13in x 7in.

I could devote a whole book to some counties. In fact, I could compile a whole book on just one place, yet there is such a small contribution from the coast of West Sussex. This book is just a collection of artwork put into some semblance of order and it has been difficult to retrieve any work from this area. There are also many places that have not been mentioned but could well appear in a future volume. Shown here is a much changed foreshore on the River Arun at Littlehampton. In contrast, the view of Bosham is an almost unchanged scene from the past hundred years.

The Quayside, Bosham. Pencil, 9in x 6in.

Repairing boats, Littlehampton. Pencil, 9in x 12in.

... and into Hampshire, Portsmouth and Southampton

H.M.S. Agamemnon *leaving Portsmouth 1784. Sepia/pencil, 17in x 10in.*

Westward off Cowes, the Solent c1920. Water-colour, 14in x 9in.

This is the *Westward*, an impressive 338-ton schooner built in 1910. She sailed in the British regatta circuit in the 1920s, known as the Big Class. Her main rival was *Britannia* and she competed against the 'J' class yachts during the 1930s.

I had always visited the Portsmouth area more to watch than record and this is, sadly, reflected in my sketch-books. I have made an exception with the *Victory*, an outstanding part of our preserved maritime history. Along with the *Warrior* and *Mary Rose* it makes Portsmouth a Mecca for enthusiasts of naval history and the sea in general. These vessels are set amongst magnificent naval buildings, some now museums, and contrast dramatically with the ever present navy of today.

H.M.S. Victory *at sea 1805 (detail). Water-colour, 26in x 18in.*

To contrast against my recent work I've included the sepia drawing of the 64-gun ship H.M.S. *Agamemnon* sailing out of Portsmouth on her maiden voyage in 1784. Said to be Nelson's favourite, this ship was built just a few miles from Portsmouth at the now preserved ship-building village of Bucklers Hard on the River Beaulieu. As research I went along to Bucklers Hard to view the slipway and take in the atmosphere, and ended up doing most of my sketching in the fascinating museum. I made a few notes from the superb models, a collection I would have loved to have in my studio! Also in the museum was a perfect diorama of Bucklers Hard, just as it would have looked in its heyday. Coincidentally, about a year after this visit I received a commission from a client in a nearby village, and discovered during conversation that not only was he a famous car modeller, a model boat-builder, an engineer and perfectionist, but he had actually made this model!

Study, H.M.S. Warrior. *Pencil, 5in x 6in.*

Study, H.M.S. Victory. *Pencil and wash, 7in x 5in.*

I have travelled the Solent both by yacht in recent years and some time ago in a merchant ship. Seven years ago whilst on a Solent 'cruise' I had the good fortune to see a renovated 'J' class yacht and the *QE2*, both queens of the sea, passing each other on the approaches to Southampton. Recently, while on a family holiday and quite by chance, I saw the *QE2* again berthed in Southampton. Making for the vantage point at the end of Hythe Pier, I was able to see this wonderful vessel take on board passengers for her next cruise. We all went on the local ferry across to Southampton and back to get some terrific views of this ship, only just painted in her new colours. Back on the pier we waited until she set sail with her accompanying flotilla of tugs and small boats in what became a party atmosphere even for those just watching. The person next to me had just that day disembarked the *QE2* and was quite excitedly filming this final farewell to make his cruise complete. Without doubt this beautiful vessel is inspirational and I felt driven to capture her on paper – no easy task as modern vessels pose a real challenge. As we all watched the *QE2* get underway and sail out of sight, I'm sure our dreams went with her.

QE2 *berthed at Southampton. Sepia, 11in x 7in.*

H.M.S. Warrior, *Portsmouth 1990. Sepia, 16in x 10in.*

Boat sketch, Bucklers Hard. Pencil, 8in x 4in.

Sketches, Portsmouth and Bucklers Hard. 15in x 10in.

Messing about, Mudeford. Pen and ink, 9in x 5in.

Frigate off Southsea c1800. 7in x 7in.

. . . and on to Dorset, Poole to Portland

Old Harry Rocks. Water-colour, 19in x 12in.

Poole has a wonderful natural harbour, with the clutter of all types of leisure and commercial boats all resulting in a charming panorama from the revamped quayside. One glorious day, I went out on a boat trip to see and sketch Old Harry Rocks and on my return saw a vessel making for the harbour with just staysails set. I was back on the shore ready for it to berth, but in what seemed no time at all the barque had all its sails furled and steamed in under power. It performed a three-point turn and tied up with no fuss at all – not quite what I expected. The local pleasure boats carried on just as normal, almost being a hindrance, as I've shown in the small water-colour. The last time I was here I had the opportunity to examine the *Maris Assumpta* at the quayside, but sadly this vessel is no longer with us.

Quayside, Poole. Water-colour, 11in x 8in.

Poole fishermen. Pen and ink, 15in x 8in.

Swanage Pier. Sepia, 10in x 5in.

Cliff study, Durlston. Pencil, 7in x 7in.

Coastal cliffs, Durlston. Water-colour, 12in x 8in.

I mentioned Old Harry Rocks earlier, and it is from here westwards that the English coastline is soft, unspoilt and at its best. Certainly Swanage, Weymouth and Lyme Regis are 'resorts' but they are small and essentially in keeping with this natural coastline. I've had summer holidays down here and found plenty of sketch-book material to feature in this book, along with the imagined sepia drawings with which comparisons can be made.

Obviously, the best vantage point for painting many coastal landmarks would seem to be in a boat just offshore. Over the years I've attempted a few as shown here. I've discovered that the instability and discomfort make it difficult and it is a challenge for the adventurous artist, but I don't recommend it.

I've included a sketch of Swanage Pier, now in a rather sorry state but still being used as a landing stage. I hope that if and when it's renovated to its former glory I can paint a comparison.

Just round from Swanage Bay is Durlston Bay and Durlston Head, and the start of the Dorset Coastal Path. This path takes in many coastal gems up to Bowleaze Cove near Weymouth. Returning to Durlston on the Purbeck coast I must mention the famous Tilly Whim Caves, and further west Whinspit. Purbeck stone is now transported from the quarries by road and has been for the last sixty years I believe, but previously the stone blocks were quarried here, brought out right on the edge of the coast and lowered by crane or derrick some forty feet onto a waiting barge, before being rowed out half a mile or so and transferred to a waiting sailing ship. Having been transferred several times at sea from boat to ship via a pilot ladder myself, at times in difficult seas, I find it incredible that such a feat of seamanship could have been contemplated, let alone carried out. These workings can be seen just as well from the sea as from the well marked coastal paths.

Stone workings, Durlston cliffs. Water-colour, 12in x 14in.

Cove near Durdle Door. Water-colour study, 10in x 7in.

Weymouth Harbour 1995. 16in x 7in.

Durdle Door, Portland Bill in the background. Water-colour, 10in x 4in.

Another resort whose fine beach has blended well with commerce, fishing and yachting is the colourful and busy harbour of Weymouth. Again, I've drawn another spectacular-looking cross-channel ferry at its berth near the harbour entrance. They seem so unreal and futuristic when viewed from a small boat. The sepia drawing overleaf is a view from the town bridge looking seawards to the sharp bend in the harbour, and with a variety of sailing traders on the River Wey, the background is very similar to today. There are no steamers in the scene and therefore it is dated sometime in the nineteenth century, a little further back in time than I intended. There is a long established trade and ferry service between this port and the Channel Isles and I can quote that even in 1951 'over 700,000,000 tomatoes were landed at Weymouth'.

Weymouth Harbour, early eighteenth century. Sepia, 12in x 9in.

I decided, on the same trip, to visit the famous Bill of Portland. Leaving the throngs of holidaymakers and picturesque harbour behind, I approached gloomy Fortuneswell with inspiration waning. However, my ascent to the hilltop above was rewarded with wonderful views all around. You can see the distinctive Chesil Beach sweeping westwards with its vast breakwater of stones, and eastwards to St Alban's Head. I will visit the famous quarries another day to draw. This 'island' is like a huge wedge and slopes down gradually to the Bill of Portland with its massive stone lighthouse, and if you walk down to the enormous boulders on the water's edge you can witness the dramatic flow of tidal water called the 'race of Portland'.

Weymouth Harbour study. Water-colour, 5in x 7in.

Bill of Portland. Water-colour, 9in x 10in.

Study of Dorset waves. Sepia, 10in x 7in.

Boat study near Bridport. Sepia, 8in x 3in.

. . . moving west into Devon, from Sidmouth to Plymouth

Shipping on the Exeter canal c1885. Sepia, 11in x 7in.

Beach study near Sidmouth. Water-colour, 10in x 7in.

Devon is so rich in coastal interest that, as with many English counties, it is difficult to do it justice in one brief chapter. However, over the years many locations have been of special interest to me.

Like many people I have visited Devon again and again, always compelled to return and always finding something new.

The water-colour of Sidmouth foreshore, a quiet sedate resort set between towering cliffs, was painted over twenty years ago at the start of my artistic career. Throughout my career my fascination for the south-west has not diminished. The sepia drawing on the title page shows shipping at Exeter at the start of the canal connecting Exeter to the River Exe.

Lynmouth Harbour. Water-colour, 8in x 10in.

Lympstone and Topsham are two little gems on the eastern side of the River Exe and these drawings, done some time apart, reveal only a little of this quiet estuary. Nothing changes too much down here and I don't know how long the 'tug' had been at Topsham but I joined two other 'Brothers of the brush' in recording it, on a late sunny afternoon.

At Lympstone, little can have changed over the last century, apart from a small harbour wall and hard standing for local pleasure boats. Of course, many of the local dwellings now provide ideal holiday homes with panoramic views over the river. In the small pencil drawing, St Peter's clock tower dominates the scene, but a century ago, or even less, the few remaining poles in the foreground would have had lines strung between them, draped with the nets of the local fishermen.

Tug at Topsham. Water-colour, 7in x 8in.

Same tug, another view. Water-colour, 8in x 6in.

On the stocks, Brixham. Pencil, 7in x 8in.

BM12

BRIXHAM - ON THE STOCKS

- LYMSTONE -

The foreshore, Lympstone. Pencil, 11in x 8in.

Inner harbour, Brixham 1993. Water-colour, 17in x 10in.

Devon's fishing history is long and varied. By the middle of the nineteenth century, not only had the Brixham fishermen established themselves in the new trawling grounds of the North Sea and their associated markets, but they had also settled in Hull, Lowestoft and other eastern fishing ports. The development of the powerful trawler and its success as a large ubiquitous fishing boat made Brixham a leading port of the time, and the move to new grounds gave rise to the new fleets that emulated them. The registration DH (the Brixham trawlers that reached Hull were registered at Dartmouth) would have been seen in all the east coast ports that fished the North Sea grounds and consequently prospered. Brixham now has an established modern stable fishing industry, mainly harvesting England's southern waters of the Channel and Western Approaches.

The pencil drawing of Brixham in readiness for a water-colour is from the early nineties, but the background has changed little over the last hundred years. Only now there are dormer windows, colourful paintwork, pleasure boats and the *Golden Hind* to make Brixham easily recognisable. Tor Bay on which Brixham nestles, in the lee of Berry Head, has always been a safe anchorage, particularly against the south-west gales. Interestingly, Brixham's tourist industry may date back to 1815 when Napoleon was captured and brought back to England by the 74-gun ship H.M.S. *Bellerophon*. It anchored in Tor Bay, just off Brixham, and when word got out the locals rowed out to see the spectacle. Was this perhaps the town's first tourist attraction?

Low tide, Brixham Harbour. Pencil, 21in x 10in.

The best views of Plymouth can be obtained from a pleasure boat around the harbour on a trip from Sutton Harbour to Devonport. Alternatively, the shores of Mount Edgecumbe Park offer a great place for a day's painting, as seen from my drawings.

To make a comparison with yesteryear, I've produced a sepia drawing of H.M.S. *Vanguard* leaving Plymouth, which was contrived from a viewpoint at Picklecombe Point, looking across to the 'Hoe' and Mountbatten Point. The small water-colour (below) was painted just further up, from Devil's Point.

Study of boats at Devonport. Pencil, 12in x 7in.

Devonport from Mount Edgecumbe Park. Water-colour, 18in x 8in.

H.M.S. Vanguard *leaving Plymouth c1800. Sepia, 19in x 11in.*

The Rivers Tavy and Tamar meet at Plymouth and then form the Hamoaze, which has the great historic naval base of Devonport on its east bank. This area has the contrasting appeal of the awesome grey warships and the masses of naval buildings on the one hand, and the green, muddy creeks and rivers on the other – a mixture of friend and foe. A slow cruise from Sutton Pier to Morwhellam Quay up the River Tamar is an ideal break from the studio for a testing but enjoyable few days' painting.

Noss Mayo. Pencil, 13in x 7in.

Brixham sailing trawler off Berry Head. Water-colour, 15in x 12in.

. . . and further west to Cornwall from Looe to St Ives

Whilst Looe is not for those seeking solitude, it is nevertheless a popular and pleasant resort relatively unsullied by constant tourist activity. It once comprised two separate communities – east and west – divided by the River Looe and joined by the spectacular seven-arched stone bridge.

Of the two communities, East Looe seems the most interesting. It has a small, established fishing fleet and, unusually in England, a speciality in shark fishing. The streets are narrow and convoluted, typical of many Cornish fishing harbours. The south side of the channel is steep, rocky and wooded and would make a dramatic backdrop to any vessel making its way in or out of harbour.

Entrance to Looe Harbour 1994. Pencil, 13in x 8in.

Low tide, Polperro 1995. Water-colour, 22in x 13in.

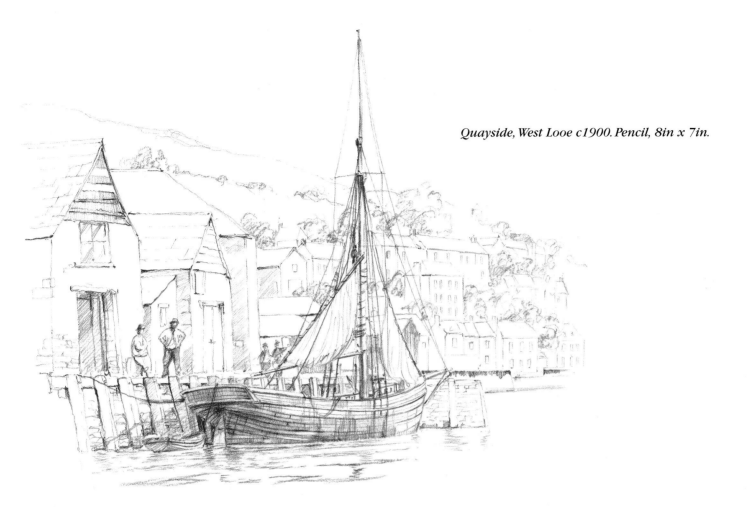

Quayside, West Looe c1900. Pencil, 8in x 7in.

Local fishermen, Coverack.
Water-colour, 12in x 9in.

Polperro is an absolute delight. It is a classic Cornish fishing village with the intrinsic natural beauty of its narrow streets of tightly packed whitewashed cottages, once all providing homes for the fisherfolk. Now, some of them house a succession of holidaymakers throughout the season. I chose the quietest spot near the harbour-side museum for both the recent very detailed water-colour and a drawing of Polperro as it would have looked in the late nineteenth century in order to demonstrate the greatest contrast. Little of the background has changed and indeed this is the feeling one gets about many Cornish ports, that the real fabric has changed little.

Although a vestigial fishing fleet exists, there are no longer any Polperro 'gaffers', as the local boats were known, in the harbour today. Polperro looks instead to the tourists for its livelihood, but the green wooded hillsides maintain the wonderfully picturesque quality of this lovely location.

Polperro 1896. Sepia, 14in x 10in.

Mousehole, early this century. Pencil, 15in x 9in.

The beach, Cadgwith. Water-colour, 9in x 10in.

Harbour study. Pencil, 9in x 11in.

The harbour, Mullion Cove.
Water-colour, 11in x 9in.

Colourful Fowey is situated on a hillside overlooking a fine natural estuary formed by coastal submergence. The River Fowey has for nearly two centuries provided the artery of trade for what is now the only commercial mineral of Cornwall, china clay, formed from the decomposition of local granite.

Pencil studies, Fowey. 15in x 11in.

Although Mevagissey faces east and therefore has some natural protection from south-west gales, it is actually a man-made fishing port with an inner and outer harbour and in its heyday would have sheltered a large fishing fleet. As with many of the Cornish fishing villages, the fishing industry has given way to tourism, with throngs of visitors drawn to the lovely buildings and steep hillsides overlooking the harbour. The fishing boats have been replaced by leisure craft.

I spent some time here drawing the inner harbour and its indigenous vessels over two tides, and still omitted much in the way of boats and clutter. The time spent there allowed me to decide on a late sun to lend atmosphere to the painting. I find it's often a good idea to view a potential subject through different 'lights' and observe the changes in colour they bring about. This painting, begun in the warm sun of a Cornish afternoon, was finished in the studio along with a pencil drawing from the same spot of an imagined but comparable scene a century ago.

Like most artists, I used to compile sketches and make observations, particularly of the light and its effects in order to undertake such detailed paintings as the one of Mevagissey, which took many hours of work and required a good deal of patience and application. However, I also make use of a camera and camcorder and appreciate the value of these aids, especially in recording what may be a momentary event and would recommend their use in a compilation of reference material.

Inner harbour, Mevagissey. Pencil study c1890, 21in x 14in.

Mevagissey Harbour 1995. Water-colour, 8in x 11in.

Fisherman, Mevagissey inner harbour. Water-colour, 8in x 7in.

Coverack Harbour, pencil study. 15in x 9in.

I have included a sketch of Falmouth dry-dock as a personal indulgence. I have great nostalgia for the scene here of the very dock where I joined ship and spent my first two weeks 'sea time' as a first trip Third-mate back in 1969. I clearly remember standing on the dock bottom, checking sea-valves and examining the miles of anchor cable laid out just as in this drawing. Absolutely nothing seems to have changed in the space of almost thirty years (almost in contradiction to what I've emphasised in this book). The dockside cranes, the tugs, the sea wall and all the bits and pieces set in the magnificent scenery of this natural harbour are all just the same as they were then.

Dry-dock, Falmouth. Pencil, 10in x 12in.

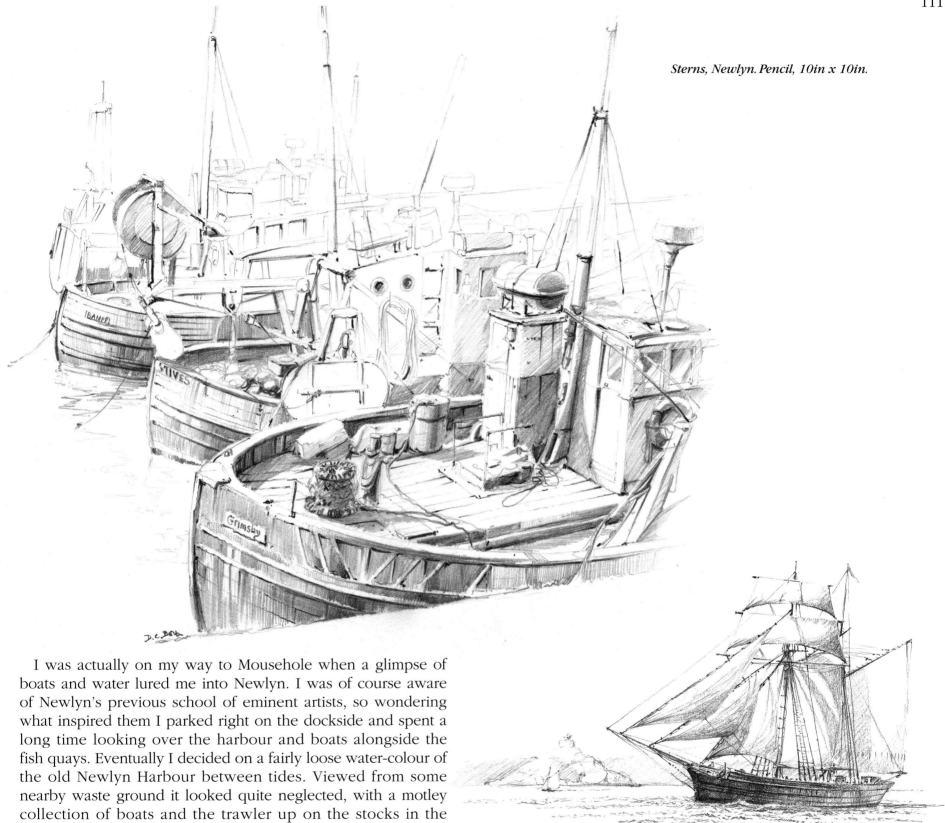

Sterns, Newlyn. Pencil, 10in x 10in.

Traders off St Michael's Mount c1890. Pencil, 9in x 6in.

I was actually on my way to Mousehole when a glimpse of boats and water lured me into Newlyn. I was of course aware of Newlyn's previous school of eminent artists, so wondering what inspired them I parked right on the dockside and spent a long time looking over the harbour and boats alongside the fish quays. Eventually I decided on a fairly loose water-colour of the old Newlyn Harbour between tides. Viewed from some nearby waste ground it looked quite neglected, with a motley collection of boats and the trawler up on the stocks in the background – all the ingredients for a good painting. Unfortunately, I was interrupted by the arrival of what seemed to be a Cornish monsoon, so after a little studio work I've included it here.

Old harbour, Newlyn. Water-colour, 20in x 11in.

A long way from my home in rural Lincolnshire, St Ives, like Newlyn, offers a wealth of subject matter for any aspiring artist. It's true the light does have a tremendous clarity, especially after a clearing downpour. The dramatic change of scene from high to low tide creates endless shapes and shadows from the dozens of ropes, boats and people tucked in by the old sea wall. The harbour has, undoubtedly, tremendous appeal, a fact illustrated by the number of artists and easels about at the time. This painting shows what St Ives Harbour was like some time ago with its distinctive fishing craft. To prepare this painting I went out of season to be sure of a parking spot. On a damp, still, early morning when the pier was quiet and deserted, I decided on the attractive central boat straight away and moved the left boat in a little to contrast with the white paintwork and deep shadows. I just picked about with the rest of the boats and tried to put in only a little of the background. With paintings like this the very fine details, and I am one for details, are usually put in later in the studio, and I spend the time on site getting the foundations and feel for the painting right. Success is not always guaranteed.

Low tide, St Ives. Water-colour, 14in x 17in.

St Ives harbour c1900. Sepia, 15in x 10in.

Harbour study, St Ives. Ink and wash, 14in x 6in.

Lizzie *ashore, St Ives. Pencil, 8in x 6in.*

Under repair, Newlyn 1995. Pencil, 10in x 6in.

. . . and finally the North-West from Fleetwood to Maryport

Trawler Daystar *leaving Fleetwood. Sepia, 12in x 7in.*

Fisherman at Whitehaven. Sepia, 12in x 7in.

Fish quay, Workington. Pencil, 9in x 5in.

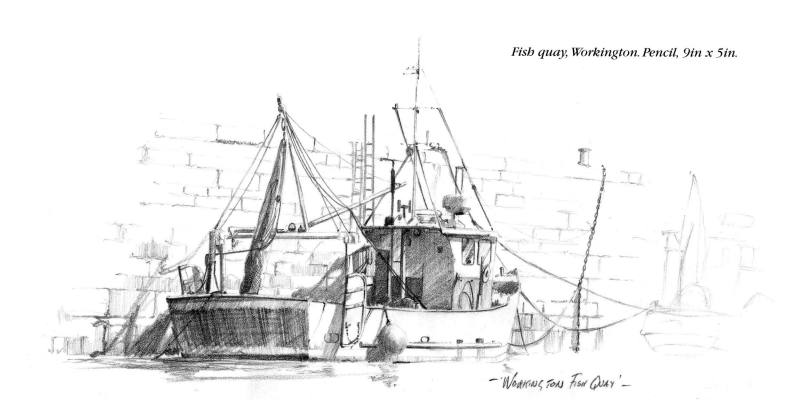

Pen studies, Fleetwood. 11in x 12in.

I couldn't quite bring myself to include Blackpool Tower, and decided on the less fashionable port of Fleetwood to start this final chapter. Though I had been to Fleetwood to visit the fish dock some years ago, I had little to show for it in preparing this chronicle of my journeys around the coast. Purposefully, therefore, I revisited the area to capture on paper some feeling of the coast.

Here are some sketches which to me show the enormous change that has been made to the number of vessels working out of this port. The fishing fleet is like a smaller 'west coast' version of Hull, with deep-water trawlers fishing Arctic waters. Near the entrance to the fish dock is the tiny Knott End Ferry which plies the River Wyre to the Fleetwood quayside where trading vessels would once have tied up to a stone quay. However, apart from the fishing boats, ferries like the huge catamaran shown here and further up the roll-on roll-off container ships are the only vessels to be seen working here on a regular basis.

I still found the shores of Fleetwood quite interesting, with a busy and varied traffic contending with an extremely fast-flowing and dangerous river. As a contrast, I've produced the sepia drawing, based on the trawler *Daystar*, leaving Fleetwood and showing just how close ships can sail past the shingle beach. I have also included what sketches I have of boats on the shoreline around the waters of Barrow and Piel Island. They indicate that I should make more visits to this interesting coastline.

A summer visitor, Fleetwood. Pen and ink, 11in x 6in.

Ravenglass, River Esk estuary. Water-colour,
12in x 8in.

Whitehaven Harbour, pencil study. 8in x 7in.

I visited and painted the coastline's only prominent and natural feature, the huge sandstone cliffs of St Bee's Head, from a southerly aspect. Even on this sunny afternoon there was little if any human activity. I then went to the north side to find another viewpoint and came upon the fascinating port of Whitehaven.

Built by the local colliery owner to serve the local coal fields, Whitehaven was once a major port of Britain with its shipbuilding and export of coal. Now, this extensive and complex system of piers and quays is intact, but little used, though a marina and its leisure craft are making an impact. I arrived a little before low-tide and apart from the excessive amount of oil in the harbour doing its best to damage my senses, I found a semi-derelict fishing boat against the quayside to start recording. Full of interest as my sketch-book will testify, the area is a little forlorn now but a complete revamp of the area is obviously underway and will make this historic area far more accessible and appealing.

Fisherman study, Whitehaven Harbour. Water-colour, 8in x 7in.

Pencil study, Ravenglass. Pencil, 8in x 6in.

122

Beach study. Water-colour, 11in x 7in.

ST. BEES CUMBRIA

St Bee's Head. Water-colour, 18in x 7in.

Harbour study, Maryport. Water-colour, 10in x 6in.

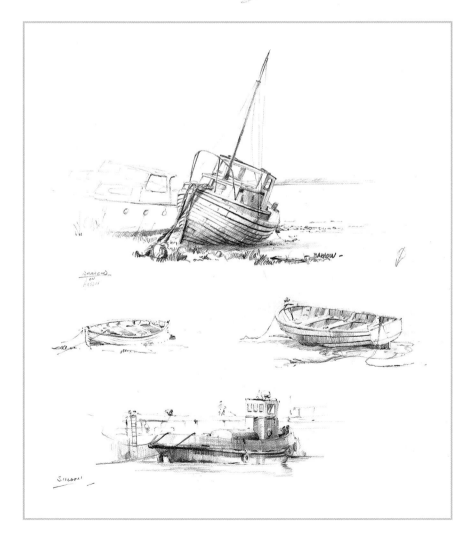

As the name suggests, Maryport was named after the wife of the local landowner and developer Humphrey Senhouse. The port is basically made up of two docks, the Senhouse Dock and the Elizabeth Dock, named after his daughter. Like Whitehaven to the south, Maryport was built as an artificial port to serve the export of local minerals and the Cumbrian speciality of iron rails. The harbour is apparently completely intact but abandoned by shipping and deserted. The maritime museum, once the harbour-side pub, is small but full of interest, and with the new marina and careful peripheral renovation, this port will attract visitors and keep its heritage alive. What better way to end this book than with a drawing to show a fully-rigged ship entering the harbour in its heyday.

Pencil sketches, coast and river. 11in x 12in.

Harbour entrance, Maryport c1885. Sepia, 6in x 11in.